Committees &
Boards

Committees & Boards

How to Be an Effective Participant

Alice N. Pohl

NTC Business Books
a division of *NTC Publishing Group* • Lincolnwood, Illinois USA

About the Author

From her many years of experience as teacher and con-
sultant, Alice N. Pohl has acquired a practical insight into
the questions and problems confronting all types of organizations regarding parliamentary procedure.

Pohl is the Accrediting Director for the American
Institute of Parliamentarians. She is the author of several
books and a variety of articles on parliamentary
procedure.

Published by NTC Business Books, a division of NTC Publishing Group.
© 1990 by NTC Publishing Group, 4255 West Touhy Avenue,
Lincolnwood (Chicago), Illinois 60646-1975 U.S.A.
Manufactured in the United States of America.
Library of Congress Catalog Card Number: 89-63137

0 ML 9 8 7 6 5 4 3 2 1

Contents

Chapter 1   Committees   1

Kinds of Committees   2
Committee Functions   2
Committee Size   3
Selecting Committees   4
　Appointment by the Chair   4
　Nomination by the Chair   4
　Nomination from the Floor   5
　As Part of the Motion Naming
　the Committee   5
　Nomination by Ballot   5
Conducting Committee
Business   6
　Rules Governing Committees   6
　Agendas   7
Committee Members   7
　Ex-Officio Members   8
　Observers   8
Discharging Committees   9

**Chapter 2   The Committee
　　　　　Chair   11**

The Effective Committee
Chair   11
Responsibilities of the Chair   12
Rules Regarding Committee
Chairs   13

**Chapter 3 Ordinary
            Committees 15**

Standing Committees 15
  Budget Committee 16
Special Committees 18
  Subcommittees 18
  Advisory Committee 19
  Nominating Committee 19
  Auditing Committee 20
  Credentials Committee 21

Chapter 4 Boards 23

Establishing the Board of
Directors 23
How Boards Function 24
Responsibilities of the Board 24
Board Officers 25
Conducting Board Meetings 26
  Agendas 26
  Other Materials 27
  Small Boards 28
Meeting by Telephone 28
Board Reports 29

**Chapter 5 The Committee
            Report 31**

Preparing Reports 31
Written Reports 32
Oral Reports 33
Presenting Reports 34
The Minority View 34
Disposition of the Report 35

Chapter 6   Motions   *37*

  Kinds of Motions   37
  Main Motions   38
  Resolutions   39
    Courtesy Resolution   40
  Subsidiary Motions   41
  Precedence of Motions   41

**Appendix   Handbook of Useful
          Motions   47**

Index   83

Chapter 1

Committees

A *committee* is a small group of one or more persons appointed or elected by an organization. The purpose of a committee is to consider, to investigate relevant matters, to report facts or findings to the assembly, or to take action.

Through committees, the activities of an organization are accomplished. Committees differ widely as to the duties or powers entrusted to them. They promote the official programs of the organization and undertake the various technical aspects of efficient club work.

Committees can make many contributions to an organization. If properly selected and oriented, committees can relieve officials of many of the details of carrying on the activities of the organization. Committees permit wider participation of an organization's members, and a greater sense of commitment to the organization. Through their contacts outside the organization, committee members can provide means to accomplish the goals of the organization. Finally, committees also provide an excellent training ground for new leaders.

Committees & Boards: How to Be an Effective Participant is designed to help readers use parliamentary procedure to most effectively participate in ordinary committees and in boards, both as officers and as members of an organization.

Kinds of Committees

Committees are divided into two classes. *Ordinary committees* are usually appointed to study, deliberate, investigate, or work for the organization. They are further subdivided into *standing* or *special* committees. Standing committees are listed in the bylaws of the organization, while special committees are elected or appointed when special needs arise.

The second class of committees is *boards*. Boards usually consist of elected representatives of the organization. The members usually are known as directors, the cabinet, the council, managers, trustees, or governors of the organization. Because the roles and operations of boards are specialized, their workings are treated in a separate chapter.

Committee Functions

Committees must know what their exact functions are. The secretary or presiding officer should give members specific instructions about their goals and responsibilities.

The preliminary information that committees should have includes the following:

– Name of committee

– Type of committee (standing or special)

– Purpose of committee, specific duties and responsibilities

– Names of chair and other members

– Time of reporting (monthly, year-end)

– Budget amount allowed

– Coordination with other committees (list special interest committees that may be working on matters related to the work of the committee; include chair's name, address, and phone number)

– Other materials and references that may be of value to the committee

Committee Size

The size of a committee depends on the task or purpose assigned to it. If the purpose of the committee requires wide representation, the committee could be larger. If the purpose of the committee is to address a relatively small task, the committee might consist of only three or four persons. The major reason for appointing a committee is the efficiency and flexibility of a smaller group. Size, therefore, should be determined by the minimum number of persons needed to accomplish the committee's purpose.

Selecting Committees

If a motion is made to refer a matter to a committee, the presiding officer should ask how the committee should be obtained. There are five methods of selecting committees: appointment by the chair; nomination by the chair; nomination from the floor; nomination by ballot; and as part of the motion naming the committee. After methods have been suggested by the members, the presiding officer calls a vote. The first method to receive a majority affirmative vote is used. If only one method for obtaining a committee is suggested, it is used without a vote unless an objection is raised.

If a committee member resigns after being elected or appointed, the vacancy must be filled by the same method used to originally establish the membership of the committee.

Appointment by the Chair

The presiding officer may appoint the members of a committee. This method is most often used. The members that are appointed are not subject to amendment or vote.

The first member named by the presiding officer is generally considered the chairperson of the committee. If the first appointee declines the position of chair, it is the duty of that person to call a meeting of the committee and act as temporary chair until the permanent chair is selected.

Nomination by the Chair

The presiding officer may nominate committee members. A vote is then taken on the group collectively.

Before the vote is taken, a member can move to amend the nominations by striking the names of certain members. If the amendment is adopted, the presiding officer nominates another to fill the vacancy. A majority vote elects the members of the committee.

Nomination from the Floor

Nominations for committee members may be made from the floor. A member need not be recognized by the chair to make a nomination, and no second is required. If more are nominated than are needed on the committee, the presiding officer calls for a vote on each nomination in order, and those who receive a majority vote are declared elected. If there are remaining nominees, they are not voted on.

If only three members are nominated for a committee requiring only three members, those persons are declared members of the committee without a vote, unless an objection is raised.

As Part of the Motion Naming the Committee

The member who makes the motion to refer a matter to committee may at the same time propose the members of the committee. This motion may be amended.

Nomination by Ballot

Nominations for a committee can be made by ballot. Under this method, each voting member receives a ballot.

Each member writes a nominee's name on the ballot. If there are more nominees than are needed, a vote can be taken to elect the number required.

Conducting Committee Business

A committee has only the power granted to it by the bylaws of the organization or given to it by the assembly. The formalities of the general assembly generally are not observed in a small committee. Matters often are discussed before they are put to the members in the form of a motion. The committee chair usually leads the discussion. He or she does not need to leave the chair in order to make a motion. However, if a committee is large, the formal rules of the assembly should be observed.

Rules Governing Committees

In a committee, questions may be discussed before a motion is made. Members do not have to rise and address the chair before speaking or making a motion, and motions do not require a second. As part of this relative informality, there is no limit on the number of times a member may speak on a question. Similarly, motions to limit or close debate are not permitted.

A motion to reconsider a question may be made by any member, even after a vote has been taken. A member who was absent when a matter was voted on may move to a reconsideration.

Committee meetings usually are confidential. Only members of the committee have the right to attend committee deliberations. Others may attend only when invited or given permission to attend.

A committee may appoint a subcommittee from its own members. The subcommittee is responsible to the committee, and not to the assembly.

Agendas

An *agenda* is a plan for addressing business. In committees, an agenda is a valuable tool for keeping the purpose of the committee in mind and for making sure that the committee's business will be completed in a timely manner.

A committee agenda should include the committee's objectives for the year, or for the period that the committee will be in existence. The agenda also should include a list of projects that will be undertaken within that time frame.

One of the most important components of a committee agenda is deadlines. Each project should have a specific culmination date. Committee members should keep these dates in mind as they go about the business.

Committee Members

Committee members should be carefully selected. The more important the committee, the more care is required.

All committee members should be genuinely interested in the business of the committee. They also should be dependable, able to accept reponsibility, and work well with other members. Working well with others involves being a good listener, being fair-minded, and being able to abide by the decision of the group.

It also is important that committee members feel that their efforts make a difference. Committee work is one of the best opportunities for members of large organizations to make a genuine, visible contribution to the business of the organization.

In addition to the regular (elected or appointed) committee members, committees may find themselves working with ex-officio members and observers.

Ex-Officio Members

If the bylaws state that the president or another officer is to be an *ex-officio member* of a committee, that person must receive notice of the meetings. An officer is made an ex-officio member by virtue of the office. For example, the treasurer of an organization may be made an ex-officio member of the finance committee, or the parliamentarian may be an ex-officio member of the rules committee. Ex-officio members have the same rights as regular members, but they are not required to attend meetings and are not counted in determining a quorum (number of members that must be present in order to conduct business).

Observers

Although meetings of a committee may not be open to members of the organization, at times it may be convenient to open the meeting, in a limited way, to members who otherwise are not eligible to attend.

When a committee is to make a decision on an important matter, it is wise to give the members of the general assembly *observer status*. The members then receive notice of the meeting and the right to attend. They have no voting rights, but if permission is given they can have an opportunity to present their views on the subject.

The observer system can be used to bring in individuals who have special knowledge about a matter the committee is considering. However, only the committee members have the right to be present during the actual deliberation of the committee.

Discharging Committees

The assembly cannot consider a question that has been referred to committee without taking the question out of the committee's hands. Normally, the committee makes its report within a specified period of time and the committee is then automatically discharged.

However, if a committee fails to make its report promptly, if it is necessary to consider a question before the committee can make its report, or if a question is to be dropped, a motion to discharge the committee may be in order.

The motion to discharge a committee cannot be made when any other question is pending. Exceptions occur when a committee has made a partial report and there is a motion either to accept the report or to accept the report and continue the committee. A motion to discharge the committee may be made as an amendment and adopted by a majority vote.

If the committee has made no report, a member may give notice that at the next meeting a motion will be made to discharge the committee. This motion requires a second and is debatable.

The motion to discharge may be amended by instructing the committee to report instead of being discharged. If previous notice has been given, the motion requires a majority vote to discharge the committee. If no notice has been given, a two-thirds vote is required.

When a committee is discharged, the chair should give the secretary all the papers relative to the subject that was entrusted to the committee.

Chapter 2

The Committee Chair

The key factor in the success of any committee's work is its chairperson. The chair must be willing to give freely of time and talent. The chair should be someone able to lead the other committee members to a successful completion of their assigned task.

The Effective Committee Chair

The chair should define the objectives of the committee. With the help of the members, the chair can outline the year's work and delegate the responsibilities to the members in relation to their skills and interests.

The chair also must make the committee members feel that they are doing the job. The chair should resist the urge to do all of the work independently. He or she also should resist the urge to assume the credit for what the committee accomplishes. When everything has been completed, credit should be given to the entire committee.

An effective committee chair stimulates others to work, is patient, does not show favoritism, and does not overload key members of the committee.

Responsibilities of the Chair

The first responsibility of the committee chair is to have a clear knowledge of the job assigned. The chair should be able to explain the primary and the lesser goals to the members.

The committee chair is responsible for calling committee meetings to order. He or she should make sure that the time and place of meetings are convenient to all members, and he or she also should make sure that all members are notified in advance and briefed on the items to be discussed. Like a presiding officer, the committee chair should prepare an agenda before the meeting and call the meeting to order on time.

If a committee chair fails to call a meeting, any two of its members should call a meeting, unless the organization's bylaws state otherwise.

The chair should keep discussion under control, talking to the entire group and calling on everyone for possible solutions. The chair should make sure each speaker is heard and understood, and that no one dominates the discussion. If tasks have been assigned to individual members, the chair should keep up-to-date on the individuals' progress. Finally, the chair should try to keep conflicts between individuals to a minimum.

It is important for a committee chairperson to maintain a positive approach. It is often helpful to discuss why each problem has to be solved, in case committee members are uncertain about the issues. Solutions should be acceptable to all. This often means not rushing the discussion and taking time to consider alternatives.

When a solution has been reached, the chair should get a verbal commitment to the solution from each member of the committee. A commitment given in the presence of others is often more binding. In small committees, the chair acts as secretary by keeping informal notes of the discussion. Based on these notes, the chair should prepare a report of the committee's activities and solutions and present the report to the assembly as required.

Rules Regarding Committee Chairs

The committee chair cannot remove other members from the committee, for example, for not attending meetings, unless the chair appointed those members. However, the chair may ask members to resign from the committee.

If a committee chair resigns, a new chair usually is appointed by the authority that established the committee and authorized the chair. For example, if the chair was appointed by the president of the organization, the president should appoint a new chair. However, if a new chair is not appointed within a reasonable amount of time by the proper authority, the committee may elect its own chair.

Chapter 3

Ordinary Committees

There are two kinds of ordinary committees. Standing committees are provided for in the bylaws of an organization. Special committees are appointed or elected as special needs arise.

Standing Committees

The bylaws of an organization provide for *standing committees*. The number and kind of standing committees depend on the size and the activities of the organization. The members of a standing committee serve for a term corresponding to that of the officers. They continue their duties until their successors have been chosen. The chair of a committee usually is appointed by the president. The members are selected on the basis of their qualifications for the particular work of the committee.

Budget Committee

In most organizations, one of the most important standing committees is the *budget committee*. The budget committee works closely with all other committees to make sure that the financial resources of the organization are directed into the overall work of the organization.

The budget committee is responsible for preparing the budget of the organization. The budget should be based on the maximum needs of the overall program. In order to arrive at a fair and workable budget, the committee should review the estimated and actual expenses for at least two preceding years; examine and analyze the organization's financial policies; receive full information on the financial requirements of the year's activities from each officer and committee chair; and include all program plans that require expenditures. A sample budget form is provided in Figure 3.1.

The *income budget* is prepared first. All sources of income should be included:

- Dues (based on actual, not estimated, figures)

- Conservative estimate of income expected from other sources

- Funds to be collected from contributions to special projects

- Any previous balance from the budget (unless such money is to be set aside as a contingency fund)

- Special or dedicated funds for special projects (these must be kept separate from general funds)

The *estimated expenditures* are prepared next. They should be based on a sound distribution of available funds. The expense budget may be broken down into several major headings. An unallocated amount should be indicated so that new or emergency projects can be carried out.

Figure 3.1

Sample Budget

Estimated Income	
Dues ___ Members @ _____	_____
Other sources of income	_____
	_____
Total anticipated income	_____
Unexpected from previous term	_____
Total available for budgeting	=======
Estimated Expenditures	
Dues to parent organization ___ members @ _____	_____
List of officers' expenses	_____
	_____
Other expenses	_____
	_____
Miscellaneous	_____
Total anticipated expenditures	_____
Unappropriated balance (emergencies)	_____
Total	=======

When the budget has been completed, it is presented to the organization for adoption or revision. The budget may be considered item by item. A budget requires a majority vote for adoption.

The budget committee cannot recommend expenses in excess of the income and expect to make up the deficit by raising dues. A raise in dues is handled according to the bylaws, and previous notice usually must be given.

Special Committees

A *special committee*, often called an *ad hoc committee*, is a committee appointed or elected to do a specific job. When the committee has completed its task and has given its final report, it is automatically discharged.

A special committee is created by means of a motion. The motion should include the method of selecting the committee, the number of members to be on the committee, and the instructions to the committee. The committee should be appointed to do a specific task.

Subcommittees

Any committee may create a *subcommittee* consisting of its own members to deal with a special aspect of the work of the committee. The subcommittee functions on behalf of the parent committee and is accountable to it.

A subcommittee is an informal group and usually is not given any official recognition by the organization. A subcommittee, unless otherwise provided for, terminates automatically when the term of the parent committee expires.

A *joint committee* is a subcommittee containing representatives of two or more organizations. A joint committee may be established for services that can be more effectively administrated over a wider area than that controlled by a single organization.

Advisory Committee

When there is a need for volunteer assistance in the work of an organization, the board of directors or the executive committee may establish an *advisory committee* or an *advisory council*. The advisory committee generally consists of leaders from professions or representatives of the general public who have made outstanding contributions in their fields. They are appointed as a consultative group. Advisory committees may provide information or otherwise assist the organization in connection with its activities. The committee's actions are not binding on the organization.

Nominating Committee

A *nominating committee* usually is a special committee, although some organizations may establish nominating committees as standing committees. Nominating committees are elected or appointed to nominate persons for offices in an organization. Members on the nominating committee should represent the various interest groups in the organization. The president should have no part in the selection of the committee, nor be an ex-officio member of it.

Nominating committees are responsible for selecting the most capable individuals for each position. They should carefully consider each candidate's dedication to the goals of the organization; how he or she relates to others; and whether he or she is likely to have the time to devote to the office. A candidate must be contacted while the committee is still in session to make sure she or he will serve if nominated and elected. The committee then puts forth the candidate's name at the appropriate general meeting of the organization.

Auditing Committee

Organizations are concerned about the way their funds are handled. The treasurer's account should be audited at least annually to protect the officers as well as the organization. While some organizations have their books audited by professional auditors, or by certified accountants who may or may not be members of the organization, other organizations appoint an *auditing committee*.

For an audit, the auditing committee needs:

- Copies of the bylaws and standing rules that specify the responsibilities and authority of the treasurer

- The treasurer's books, cancelled checks, receipts, vouchers, current bank statement, and other memos

- Copies of the secretary's minutes documenting authorization for payment of bills

- The budget

Generally, an auditing committee begins by comparing the bank statement at the end of the previous year with the current year's beginning balance. Then total bank deposits are added and total checks paid are deducted. The resulting balance should be the same as the closing bank statement. All cash receipts are then checked to make sure they agree with the bank deposits. Finally, the minutes are examined for approval of payment of bills.

The bank statement, deposits, and paid bills should all agree. If there is a difference, the treasurer should be asked to explain the difference before the auditing committee's report is made.

Credentials Committee

A *credentials committee* is responsible for determining and organizing the representation for a convention. Credentials committees generally are appointed by the president or the executive committee.

Before any convention, the credentials committee provides constituent bodies of the organization with information about how many delegates and alternates the body is entitled to, the eligibility requirements, and the time and manner of their election. Delegates and alternates are required to return credential forms in advance of the convention (see Figure 3.2).

One or two days before the convention opens, the credentials committee supervises *registration*. Registrants present evidence that they are entitled to vote. The credentials committee verifies the members' credentials by checking the credential form files; records their registration; and provides the members with badges, programs, or other necessary materials.

Based on the registration, the credentials committee makes its report as the first item of official business of the convention. The report states the number of delegates with proper credentials registered at a given time.

The committee continues to serve until the end of the convention, in order to record changes in the registration of delegates, to re-register alternates who replace delegates, and to make credentials reports as needed.

Figure 3.2

Sample Credential Form

Name of Organization
Credentials of the Delegate or Alternate

Please print or type   Mail this portion

The members of _____ of _____
                      (name of organization)   (city & state)

Have elected _____ as the delegate and

_____ as the alternate to represent our

_____ at the Annual Convention _____
(club, unit, region)   (date)

Complete and Return This Half No Later Than (date)

Mail to: _____
                                      signature of delegate

                                _____
                                      signature of alternate

                                _____
                                      signature of president

Name of Organization
Credential form – Delegate or Alternate

Please print or type

The members of _____ of _____
                      (name of organization)   (city & state)

Have elected _____ as the delegate and

_____ as the alternate to represent our

_____ at the Annual Convention _____
(club, unit, region)   (date)

Delegate: Please bring   _____
this half to the convention   signature of delegate
and present it properly
signed at the credentials   _____
desk.   signature of alternate

                              _____
                                    signature of president

Chapter 4

Boards

A *board* is a group of members of an organization, elected or appointed, which is authorized to act for the organization between its meetings. Some common names for boards include: the executive board; the board of directors, governors, trustees, or managers; the cabinet; or the commission. Members of boards are commonly called *directors*.

In some organizations, the directors—other than those elected by the membership—provide for observers to the board who are nonvoting members. In addition, there may be provision for honorary directors, who generally serve in an advisory capacity.

Establishing the Board of Directors

The size of the board of directors varies greatly, depending on the kind of organization and the work involved.

In smaller organizations, the board may consist of less than twelve members. In larger organizations, the board may consist of up to forty members. The criteria for determining the makeup of the board of directors are of great importance. The bylaws of the organization should be specific as to the composition so that it will be balanced. Some organizations stagger membership in the board to prevent a majority of new members at any time.

How Boards Function

A board of directors functions in much the same way as an ordinary committee. The work of the board may be divided among a number of special or permanent committees, each dealing with some phase of the organization's objectives. These committees report back to the board, as they are subordinate to it.

A board cannot appoint an executive committee unless the bylaws so authorize. The executive committee usually is made up of the elected officers. It has the power to act for the board within limitations when the board is not meeting, but it cannot modify any action taken by the board.

Responsibilities of the Board

A board has only the authority given it by the constitution or bylaws, or voted to it by the organization. A board may be granted the power to act for the organization between meetings; however, a board's actions cannot conflict with any action taken by the organization. A board may be authorized to adopt its own rules for the conduct of its business. These rules continue to be in force until they are amended, suspended, or rescinded.

If the bylaws do not state otherwise, a quorum is a majority of the board. If the bylaws provided for a person who is not a member of the organization to be a member of the board, that person has all the rights as other members but is not counted in the quorum.

In nonprofit corporations or organizations, ordinary members may be allowed to vote by proxy. Directors or board members, however, cannot vote by proxy in their meetings. Directors have special responsibilities and powers which they cannot delegate to another individual.

A board of directors is considered to have authority only as a group. Directors as individuals have no legal power except for that delegated to them by the board. However, directors can be held liable as individuals for an action or failure to act as a board member. A board has no power to punish or censure its members. However, it can make a report to the organization.

Board Officers

The officers of the board usually are the officers of the organization, with the president and secretary serving in the same capacity. Some boards include *ex-officio* members. These persons are members of the board by virtue of holding an office or chairing a committee, or because they are members of the parent organization. If an ex-officio member is a member of the organization, he or she has the same rights and obligations as other board members.

If the immediate past president of the organization is an ex-officio member of the board, he or she holds that position until the present president becomes the immediate past president. If the immediate past president dies during his or her tenure as an ex-officio member, that office remains vacant until the current president becomes the immediate past president.

Conducting Board Meetings

Board meetings can vary in length from a few minutes to sessions that seem to end only when each person reaches the point of sheer physical exhaustion. Usually, business in large boards is transacted according to the rules of the assembly. The business should be within the scope and purpose of the organization, unless the bylaws state otherwise.

Agendas

In preparing for a board meeting, the presiding officer's purpose should be to obtain group achievements. An *agenda* should be prepared and given to members in advance of the meeting. This will make clear what subjects will be discussed and how the subjects will affect the members. An agenda should include what the meeting will be about and how long it will last.

Some presiding officers prefer to plan the entire agenda. Others will give the secretary the items of importance and let the secretary add other subjects that should be considered. A typical agenda is illustrated in Figure 4.1.

Figure 4.1

Typical Board Agenda

1. Call to order

2. Reading and approval of minutes

3. Reports of officers

4. Reports of committees

5. Special orders (business postponed to a specific time)

6. Unfinished business and general orders (business postponed to an indefinite time)

7. New business

8. Announcements

9. Closing and adjournment

The presiding officer or secretary may call those who are to attend the meeting and ask if they have anything to place on the agenda. The presiding officer or secretary also should be aware of the concerns of the members of the organization. Such items should be included as items of business. When the advance work is properly done, the board will be able to identify and pinpoint problems and to convert their plans into action.

Other Materials

It often is helpful to circulate copies of the financial statement and previous minutes to board members before each meeting. This gives members the opportunity to review the materials and prepare for discussion. It may be possible to approve the minutes as mailed, thus reducing the length of the board meeting.

Small Boards

Business in a small board should be within the scope and purpose of the organization. The agenda is the same as that of a larger board. Members need not rise to obtain the floor or to make a motion, motions need not be seconded, and there is no limit to the number of times a member can speak to a question. The motion to close debate (previous question) is not allowed.

Generally, informal discussion is permitted without a motion in small boards. If a subject is clear to everyone, it can be agreed to by general consent. Also, the presiding officer can discuss a subject without leaving the chair. However, once a motion is made, it must be voted on under the same rules as in the general assembly.

Meeting by Telephone

In cases when it is impossible to get together to take care of crisis situations, an emergency board meeting may be called by conference call. At least two-thirds of the members must be on the phone, and all formal votes must be taken by roll call. Such a meeting is followed up with the necessary paperwork to support the meeting. The record should reflect:

- Date and time of call

- Purpose of call

- Names of all members participating

- Roll-call vote

- Signature of person recording the discussion

Emergency action must be ratified at the next business meeting.

Obtaining and approving information from members of the board individually is not the same as approval of the board, since members are not together to hear the same information, discuss, and decide the matter. Even if there is unanimous agreement of the members outside of a properly called meeting, such agreement does not qualify as an act of the board.

Board Reports

The proceedings of the board must be recorded in the *minutes*. These minutes are read and approved by the board. Board minutes generally are not read to the assembly; however, a summary may be given to the assembly.

A board may present a recommendation to the assembly with a motion that it be adopted. It also may present the matter as a resolution. Usually the secretary reads the resolution. No second is required. The presiding officer may ask for discussion on the resolution.

At the annual meeting, the board makes an annual report. All unfinished business of the board dies when a new board assumes its duties.

Chapter 5

The Committee Report

Reports may be called *studies*, *surveys*, and *opinions*. They may vary in form and substance. Reports may be long or short, formal or informal, special or routine, periodic or serial; they may be typewritten, printed, or given orally.

Since much time is devoted in business meetings to hearing and considering reports, it is important that they be presented in a manner that will bring the most effective results. This chapter outlines some techniques for preparing and presenting effective committee reports.

Preparing Reports

The committee chairperson usually prepares the report and presents it to the committee for acceptance. The committee may make any necessary changes. When the report is deemed satisfactory by the majority of members, the committee adopts it.

When preparing a report, there are three important things to bear in mind: purpose, scope, and audience. These three considerations govern the length, depth, and wording of the report. If the report involves a simple matter, such as the report of a minute-approving committee, the report should be simple and direct. If the report involves a relatively complex matter, such as whether the organization should make major changes in its bylaws, the report should carefully spell out the purpose and consequences of those changes.

Reports also should include the proper *tone*. All committee reports, oral or written, should be in the third person. Formal reports should be impersonal and factual. Informal reports should not be casual; they should be businesslike, stressing the subject. Long reports may be divided into parts or sections with numbered divisions.

Every report should include a clear introduction that includes a statement of the purpose and scope of the report, the method of investigation, or the details of the research. Concise background information, such as a brief history of the problem or previous studies made, also may be given.

Written Reports

Most written reports follow a standard format. They begin with the *heading*, which includes the name of the organization, the title of the report, and the date the report was adopted by the committee.

The *body* of the report follows. It includes an introductory statement, giving the purpose and reason for the report; development of the subject matter through investigation, observation, and materials used; the frequency of committee meetings; and a conclusion, which may contain a recommendation or resolution.

The report concludes with the *signature*. This normally includes simply the signature of the committee chair, with that person's name and title typed below. However, if the report is of considerable importance, all concurring members of the committee include their signatures. (If all concurring members are included, the chair typically signs first and his or her title is omitted.)

Oral Reports

Oral reports should follow the same basic format as written reports. An oral report often may be accompanied by written copies of the report for the official record or even for the members.

It is important to prepare adequately for an oral report. It may be helpful to prepare an outline or speaking notes. The person who will give the report (usually the committee chair) should review the outline or notes several times and perhaps even practice aloud. If the report contains several points or many statistics, it may be helpful to plan visual aids. The speaker should determine what kind of visuals (overhead transparencies, slides, posters, chalkboard notes) will work best in the designated meeting place.

To make an effective oral presentation, speakers should stand and look at the audience. Speakers should state the name of the committee and identify themselves. They should be sure that everyone can hear what is being said. To maintain attention, speakers should try to be positive and enthusiastic. They should have all necessary backup information on hand in order to answer questions from the audience.

Presenting Reports

Normally, either *motions* or *subjects* are referred to committees. When a committee working on a motion is ready to report, the committee chair or someone designated by the chair rises and states, "The committee to which was referred the motion ... has considered it and has an amendment (*or* substitute motion) to offer." Usually, this report can be made orally, unless the original motion, the amendment, or the substitute motion is quite long or complex.

When a committee working on a subject is ready to report, the report normally should be written. The report should begin: "The committee that was appointed to investigate ... and to make recommendations, submits the following report." The report ends with: "In conclusion, the committee recommends the adoption of the following: RESOLVED, That ...."

The Minority View

Official committee reports present the majority view of the committee. Members of the committee who disagree with the report also may submit their views, although they must do this separately.

After the committee report is presented, the reporting member may say that the minority would like to present its view. The presiding officer may state that the minority view will be heard if there is no objection. If an objection is raised, a member may move that the minority view be heard.

The view of the minority should be in writing. A typical opening for a minority report follows: "The undersigned members, not agreeing with the report of the majority of the committee, submit the following report." The body of the report follows the signatures of the dissenting committee members.

If the committee report contained a resolution or recommendation, the reporting member for the minority view may move to substitute the committee resolution or recommendation with the minority resolution or recommendation.

Disposition of the Report

When the assembly hears a report, that report is *received*. The assembly can take a number of actions on a report that includes a recommendation or a resolution:

1. The report may be referred back to committee if it is not satisfactory, or if it requires further study or modification.

2. The report may be postponed to a more convenient time.

3. The report may be adopted; an adopted report commits the assembly to all findings contained in the report.

4. The report may be adopted in part with exceptions; any resolution or motion in the report may be

amended, although the report itself cannot be amended unless it contains misinformation.

5. The report may be rejected.

Reports containing information are filed, not adopted. A filed report is not binding on the assembly; it is simply available for information.

Chapter 6

Motions

Business is transacted in a meeting by way of motions. A member makes a proposal that is accepted or rejected. The members of the assembly may wish to defer consideration of the subject, or they may be willing to accept it with certain modifications.

Kinds of Motions

There are two kinds of motions: *main* and *secondary*. The main motion is the proposal or proposition. If the main motion is accepted, it commits the assembly to take action. The main motion has implications beyond the present meeting.

Motions are classified in the following ways:

I. Main Motions
   A. Original
   B. Specific Main Motions

II. Secondary Motions
   A. Subsidiary
   B. Privileged
   C. Incidental

The main motion brings business before the assembly. A secondary motion is a procedural motion that is made and considered while the main motion is on the floor. When a secondary motion is made, it becomes the immediately pending question, while the main motion remains pending. Certain secondary motions take priority over others. It is possible to have more than one secondary motion pending at the same time that the main motion is pending.

Main Motions

A main motion is a proposal that brings business before the assembly. The proposal is a member's request that something be done or that a statement express the sense, opinion, or wish of the assembly. As a general rule, a main motion is stated in the affirmative. It should be clear, definite, and brief. A long or complicated motion should be submitted in writing.

Parliamentary procedure governs how a motion should be presented and when it is in order. A main motion requires recognition by the chair, requires a second, is debatable, and is amendable. A main motion is not in order when another member has the floor. It yields to any subsidiary, privileged, or applicable incidental motion.

A main motion usually requires a majority vote. Exceptions to this rule include when the bylaws of the organization require a greater vote, when adoption would suspend a rule of order or a parliamentary right, or when adoption would rescind or amend something previously adopted. A main motion may be reconsidered by the assembly.

All subsidiary and privileged motions can be made while the main motion is pending. Other applicable incidental motions can be made, for example, division of the question, to consider seriatim (consider the proposition paragraph by paragraph), to withdraw, and to object to the consideration of an original main motion.

Specific main motions are motions that are incidental to or relate to the business of the assembly or to its past or future action. They usually are made orally. Some examples of specific main motions include:

- To ratify emergency action taken at a meeting when no quorum was present

- To rescind an action or rule already adopted

- To adopt a recommendation that an officer or committee has been directed to make

- To take a motion laid on the table from the table

- To amend something previously adopted

A member may object to the consideration of an original main motion, but it is not in order to object to the consideration of an incidental main motion.

Resolutions

A *resolution* is a formally written main motion. It may be a formal statement of the opinions of the assembly.

The difference between a standard main motion and a resolution is that a main motion is proposed by the words "I move that . . . ." A resolution is proposed by the words "I move the adoption of the following resolution,

Resolved, That . . . ." A resolution presented by a committee or board does not require a second, but all other rules pertaining to a main motion apply.

A resolution may have a *preamble*. A preamble consists of one or more clauses, each beginning with the word *Whereas*. The preamble is a brief statement giving the background or reasons for the motion. It presents arguments for the resolution's adoption. The preamble should contain only clauses that contain little-known information or items of unusual importance, without which the resolution is likely to be misunderstood.

The correct format for a resolution is illustrated below. In the preamble, the word *Whereas* introduces each item. It is followed by a comma. The next word begins with a capital letter, and the phrase ends with a semicolon followed by the word *and*. The last *Whereas* closes with a semicolon followed by the words *therefore be it* or simply *be it*. The beginning resolving clause begins a new line.

Whereas, A . . . ; and
Whereas, The . . .; therefore be it
Resolved, That [stating action to be taken]; and
Resolved, That [stating further action to be taken].

Each resolving clause in a resolution is voted on separately, as each is a primary motion. Each clause may be debated, amended, referred, postponed, or laid on the table. After the resolving clauses have been voted upon, the preamble is then put to a vote. Depending on the disposition of the resolving clauses, the preamble may be amended.

Courtesy Resolution

A committee is often charged with the duty of drafting and presenting to the assembly a *courtesy resolution*. Ordinarily, courtesy resolutions express the appreciation of an assembly or convention to those who arranged accommodations or rendered service. No opposing vote is taken on a courtesy resolution.

Subsidiary Motions

Subsidiary motions assist in treating or disposing of the main motion or other motions. They are used to modify, delay action on, or dispose of the pending motion. When a subsidiary motion is stated by the chair, it supersedes a pending motion of lower rank and becomes the immediately pending question.

Certain subsidiary motions may be applied to others. For example, a motion to amend may be amended, referred to a committee, or postponed. Debate on an amendment may be limited or extended by subsidiary motion.

Subsidiary motions, their purpose, and their application are discussed in depth in the Appendix "Handbook of Useful Motions," beginning on page 47.

Precedence of Motions

Before a subject can be considered, it must be brought before the assembly in the form of a motion or proposition. Only one main motion can be considered at a time. After the main motion has been stated by the chair, it must be adopted or rejected by the assembly, or the assembly must take some other action to dispose of it before any other subject can be brought up.

The consideration of a main motion may involve a number of secondary motions. Secondary motions enable an assembly to arrive at the general will of the members on a number of questions. The presiding officer is responsible for recognizing a secondary motion, its purpose, and its rank. The presiding officer should ensure that motions are handled in their proper order of precedence. Table 6.1 lists the various kinds of motions and shows their precedence.

Table 6.1

Table of Motions

Privileged Motions	Can Interrupt Speaker	Requires Second	Debatable	Amendable	Vote Required	Can Be Reconsidered
Fix the time to which to adjourn	no	yes	no	yes	majority	yes
Adjourn (unqualified)	no	yes	no	no	majority	no
Take a recess	no	yes	no	yes	majority	no
Question of privilege	yes	no	no	no	●	no
Orders of the day	yes	no	no	no	●	no
Subsidiary Motions						
Lay on the table (temporarily)	no	yes	no	no	majority	no
Previous question (stop debate)	no	yes	no	no	2/3	yes
Limit or extend debate	no	yes	no	yes	2/3	yes
Postpone to certain time	no	yes	yes	yes	majority	yes

	Can Interrupt Speaker	Requires Second	Debatable	Amendable	Vote Required	Can Be Reconsidered
Refer to committee	no	yes	yes	yes	majority	yes
Amend	no	yes	yes	yes	majority	yes
Postpone indefinitely	no	yes	yes	no	majority	aff. vote only
Main Motion	no	yes	yes	yes	majority	yes
Specific Main Motions						
Reconsider	no	yes	yes*	no	majority	no
Ratify	no	yes	yes	yes	majority	yes
Rescind	no	yes	yes	yes	(1)	neg. vote only
Take from the table	no	yes	no	no	majority	no
Discharge committee	no	yes	yes	yes	2/3	neg. vote only
Amend something previously adopted	no	yes	yes	yes	(1)	neg. vote only

* Except when the motion to be reconsidered is debatable.

• Chair usually decides. Majority if put to vote.

(1) Requires a two-thirds vote when applied to constitution, bylaws, or special rules. Requires a majority vote when notice is given at a previous meeting, or a majority vote of the entire membership without notice.

(2) If not granted by general consent, can be moved by person requesting permission.

(3) Yes, if motion made by person requesting permission.

	Can Interrupt Speaker	Requires Second	Debatable	Amendable	Vote Required	Can Be Reconsidered
Incidental Motions (no rank)						
Point of order	yes	no	no	no	•	no
Appeal from the decision of chair	yes	yes	limited	no	majority	yes
Suspend the rules of order	no	yes	no	no	2/3	no
Suspend standing rules	no	yes	no	no	majority	no
Object to consideration	yes	no	no	no	2/3	neg. vote only
Division of a question (motion)	no	yes	no	yes	majority	no
Consider by paragraph (section)	no	yes	no	yes	majority	no
Division of assembly (vote)	yes	no	no	no	none	no
Close polls	no	yes	no	yes	2/3	no

	Can Interrupt Speaker	Requires Second	Debatable	Amendable	Vote Required	Can Be Reconsidered
Reopen polls	no	yes	no	yes	majority	neg. vote only
Close nominations	no	yes	no	yes	2/3	no
Reopen nominations	no	yes	no	yes	majority	neg. vote only
Parliamentary inquiry	yes	no	no	no	none	no
Request for information	yes	no	no	no	none	no
Excused for duty	no	yes	yes	yes	majority	neg. vote only
Withdraw a motion	(1)	(2)	no	no	majority	neg. vote only
Create a blank	no	yes	no	no	majority	no
Fill a blank	no	no	yes	no	majority	yes
Request to read a paper	(1)	(2)	no	no	majority	yes
Motions relating to voting	no	yes	no	yes	majority	no

* Except when the motion to be reconsidered is debatable.

• Chair usually decides. Majority if put to vote.

(1) Requires a two-thirds vote when applied to constitution, bylaws, or special rules. Requires a majority vote when notice is given at a previous meeting, or a majority vote of the entire membership without notice.

(2) If not granted by general consent, can be moved by person requesting permission.

(3) Yes, if motion made by person requesting permission.

Appendix

Handbook of Useful Motions

This appendix covers the most commonly used motions, their purpose, and their application. The appendix is arranged in alphabetical order for easy reference.

There are two kinds of motions, *main* and *secondary.* Main motions are the motions that bring business before the meeting. Secondary motions are procedural and can be considered while a main motion is on the floor. Secondary motions are identified as subsidiary, privileged, and incidental.

Subsidiary motions are always applied to another motion while it is pending and, if adopted, always do something to this other motion. Subsidiary motions have rank. When a motion is before the meeting, any motion is in order if it has a higher precedence or rank than the immediately pending motion; no motion having a lower precedence is in order.

Privileged motions deal with special matters of immediate importance which, without debate, are allowed to interrupt the consideration of anything else. They have no bearing on the subject before the meeting.

Incidental motions apply to the method of transacting business, rather than to the business itself. They relate in different ways to the pending business and deal with questions of procedure arising out of another pending motion. Incidental motions have no rank among themselves. With few exceptions, they are related to the main question in such a way that they must be decided upon immediately, before any business can proceed.

There can be only one main motion on the floor at a time, but it is possible to have several secondary motions on the floor at the same time, provided they are made according to their rank.

Table A.1 lists the order of precedence of motions.

Table A.1

Order of Precedence of Motions—Highest to Lowest

I.   Privileged Motions
1. Fix the Time to Which to Adjourn
2. Adjourn
3. Recess
4. Question of Privilege
5. Call for the Orders of the Day

II.   Subsidiary Motions
6. Lay on the Table
7. Previous Question
8. Limit or Extend Debate
9. Postpone Definitely
10. Commit or Refer
11. Amend
12. Postpone Indefinitely

III.   The Main Motion

IV.   Specific Main Motions (no order of precedence)
Discharge a Committee
Ratify
Reconsider
Rescind
Take from the Table

V.   <u>Incidental Motions (no order of procedence)</u>

      Appeal

      Consider by Paragraph or Seriatim

      Division of a Question

      Division of the Assembly

      Motions Relating to Nominations

      Motions Relating to the Polls and Methods of
        Voting

      Motions That Are Requests

      Object to the Consideration of a Question

      Point of Order

      Suspend the Rules

      Withdraw

Adjourn

A privileged motion. This motion is made to terminate a meeting.

Forms of the Motion

"I move that we adjourn."

"I move to adjourn."

"I move that we adjourn at 8 o'clock."

"I move that when we adjourn, we adjourn to meet at the same time tomorrow evening."

Rules Governing the Motion

1. Cannot interrupt a speaker
2. Requires recognition
3. Is not debatable
4. Is not amendable
5. Requires a majority vote
6. May not be reconsidered

After the motion to adjourn has been moved, the following parliamentary steps are in order while the motion to adjourn is pending, or after the meeting has voted to adjourn:

1. Inform the members of business requiring attention before adjournment
2. Make important announcements
3. Make (but not take up) a motion to reconsider a previous vote
4. Give notice of a motion to be made at the next meeting (or on the next day of a convention) where the motion requires previous notice
5. Move to set the time for an adjourned meeting if the time for the next meeting is not already settled

The meeting is not closed until the chair has declared that the meeting is adjourned. Members should not leave their seats until the chair says, "The meeting is adjourned."

A meeting can be adjourned without a motion if the time for adjournment has arrived. The chair simply announces that the meeting is adjourned. When it appears that there is no further business, the chair may say, "There being no further business, the meeting is adjourned."

Adopt

An incidental motion. The expressions *adopt*, *accept*, and *agree to* are all equivalent. It is best to use the word *adopt*.

Forms of the Motion

"I move that we adopt the recommendation of the committee."

"I move that the auditor's report be adopted."

Rules Governing the Motion

1. Cannot interrupt a speaker

2. Requires recognition

3. Requires a second

4. Is debatable

5. Is amendable

6. Requires a majority vote

7. May be reconsidered

Amend

A subsidiary motion. This motion is made to change the wording of the motion before final action is taken on it.

There are two kinds of amendments, the primary (first degree) and the secondary (second degree) amendments. The primary amendment amends the pending motion and must be germane to it, that is, closely related to the motion. The secondary amendment amends the primary amendment and must be germane to it. Secondary amendments do not apply to the main motion. Only two amendments may be pending at one time. After they have been disposed of, another amendment may be made, if it is germane. When there are two amendments pending, the secondary amendment is voted on first, then the primary amendment. The main motion is then open for discussion before the final vote is taken.

Forms of the Motion

"I move to amend the motion by adding at the end . . . ."

"I move to amend the motion by striking out the word (or words) between . . . and . . . ."

"I move to insert the word (or words) between the word . . . and the word . . . ."

"I move to amend the motion by striking out the word (or words) and inserting the word (or words) between the word . . . and the word . . . ."

"I move to strike out the main motion and insert . . . ."

"I move to substitute the following . . . ."

Rules Governing the Motion

1. Is not in order when another has the floor

2. Requires recognition

3. Requires a second

4. Is debatable when applied to a debatable motion

5. Is amendable (a primary amendment is amendable; a secondary amendment is not)

6. Yields to higher ranking subsidiary motions and all privileged and applicable incidental motions, except motions to divide and to consider by paragraph or seriatim

7. Requires a majority vote even if the motion to be amended requires a higher vote (a primary amendment requires two votes, the first on the amendment and the second on the pending main motion; a secondary amendment requires three votes, the first on the secondary amendment, the second on the primary amendment, and the third on the pending main motion)

8. May be reconsidered

Amend Something Previously Adopted

A specific main motion. This is a motion by which an action previously adopted or taken can be changed, repealed, or annulled.

Forms of the Motion

"I move to amend the motion adopted at the January meeting by striking out.... Previous notice was given at the last meeting."

"I move to amend the motion relating to...adopted at the May meeting by inserting.... Previous notice has been given."

Rules Governing the Motion

1. Cannot interrupt a speaker

2. Requires recognition

3. Requires a second

4. Is debatable; debate may go into the merits of the motion which it is proposed to amend

5. Is amendable

6. Requires a two-thirds vote or a vote of a majority of the entire membership, except when notice has been given at a previous meeting; then the motion requires a majority vote

7. Only the negative vote may be reconsidered

Appeal

An incidental motion. This motion allows a member who disagrees with the ruling of the chair to have the assembly make the decision.

Form of the Motion

"I appeal from the decision of the chair."

Rules Governing the Motion

1. Is in order when another member has the floor; must be proposed immediately

2. Does not require recognition

3. Requires a second

4. Is debatable

5. Is not amendable

6. Requires a majority vote in the negative to overrule the chair's decision (a majority vote or tie vote sustains the decision of the chair)

7. Takes precedence over any question and must be decided immediately

Call for the Orders of the Day

A privileged motion. This motion requires that the assembly conform to its agenda, program, or order of business, or that it take up a general or special order due to come up.

When the orders of the day are called for, the chair may say, "Would the assembly care to finish this part of the business before adhering to the orders of the day?" If there is an affirmative vote, the business is completed before returning to the agenda.

Form of the Motion

"I call for the orders of the day."

Rules Governing the Motion

1. Is in order when another has the floor

2. Does not require recognition

3. Does not require a second

4. Is not debatable

5. Is not amendable

6. Upon the call by a single member, the chair must take up the prescribed order of business; no vote is necessary

7. Cannot be reconsidered

Close Debate

A subsidiary motion. This motion is to prevent or to stop discussion on the pending question or questions and to bring the pending question to an immediate vote.

Forms of the Motion

"I move to close debate on the motion."

"I move to close debate on all pending motions."

Rules Governing the Motion

1. Cannot interrupt a speaker

2. Requires recognition

3. Requires a second

4. Is not debatable

5. Is not amendable

6. Requires a two-thirds vote

7. Can be applied to debatable motions only

Close Nominations

An incidental motion. A nomination is a formal presentation of the member's name as a candidate for a particular office. When there are several candidates for an office, a member may wish to close nominations.

In cases when it appears that there are no further nominations for a particular office, the chair declares the nomination closed, or someone may move to close nominations. Usually no motion is necessary to close nominations, since they may be reopened by a motion to this effect.

Form of the Motion

"I move to close nominations."

Rules Governing the Motion

1. Cannot interrupt a speaker
2. Requires recognition
3. Requires a second
4. Is not debatable
5. Is amendable
6. Requires a two-thirds vote.

Commit *or* Refer

A subsidiary motion. This motion is made to refer a pending motion to one or more persons. This motion may be applied to a main motion or to a main motion with adhering amendments.

Forms of the Motion

"I move to refer the question to a committee."

"I move to refer the motion to the . . . committee."

"I move to refer the motion to a committee of three appointed by the chair."

"I move to refer the question to the executive committee with power to act."

Rules Governing the Motion

1. Cannot interrupt a speaker
2. Requires recognition
3. Requires a second
4. Is debatable as to the desirability of committing and
   to the appropriate details of the motion to commit
5. Is amendable as to the committee composition, manner of composition, and instructions to the committee
6. Requires a majority vote
7. Can be reconsidered if the committee has not begun
   consideration of the question

Consider Informally

A subsidiary motion. This motion allows the members to
speak informally on a motion. If this motion passes, the
question is open to informal consideration. There is no
limit to the number of times a member can speak on the
question or on any amendment. As soon as the question
has been voted upon, the informal consideration ceases.

Form of the Motion

"I move that we discuss this subject informally."

Rules Governing the Motion

1. Cannot interrupt a speaker
2. Requires recognition
3. Requires a second
4. Is debatable
5. Is not amendable
6. Requires a majority vote

Consider by Paragraph

An incidental motion. This motion provides for long motions or reports consisting of several paragraphs, resolutions, or sections to be considered by opening different parts to debate and amendment separately, without dividing the question.

Each paragraph is open to debate and amendment if the motion to consider by paragraph is adopted. When no further amendments are proposed and debate ceases on that paragraph, the chair proceeds to the next paragraph until all have been open to debate and amendment. After all paragraphs are amended, the entire series is open to further amendment and debate. At this time additional parts may be inserted or parts may be struck out. A single vote is then taken on the adoption of the entire series.

Forms of the Motion

"I move that the resolution be considered by paragraph."

"I move that the bylaws be considered by sections."

Rules Governing the Motion

1. Cannot interrupt a speaker

2. Requires recognition

3. Requires a second

4. Is not debatable

5. Is amendable

6. Requires a majority vote

7. Cannot be reconsidered

Discharge a Committee

A specific main motion. This is a motion by means of which further consideration of a subject may be taken away from a committee. The assembly can take the matter out of a committee's hands after it has been referred to it and before the committee has made a final report. So long as a question (subject) is in the hands of a committee, the assembly cannot consider another motion involving practically the same thing.

No motion is necessary to discharge a committee when the committee has given its final report to the assembly. The committee is then automatically discharged from further consideration of the matter.

Forms of the Motion

"I move that the committee to which was referred the motion regarding . . . be discharged."

"I move that the committee appointed to investigate the question of . . . be discharged and that this matter be made a special order of business at our next meeting."

"I move that the membership committee be discharged from further consideration of the motion referred to it on . . . ."

Rules Governing the Motion

1. Cannot interrupt a speaker

2. Requires recognition

3. Requires a second

4. Is debatable; debate may go into the merits of the question which is in the hands of the committee

5. Is amendable by the basic process of amending, and may instruct the committee instead of discharging it

6. Requires a two-thirds vote, or a vote of the majority of the entire membership, or only a majority vote if previous notice has been given at a previous meeting or in the call to the meeting

7. Only the negative vote may be reconsidered

Division of the Assembly

An incidental motion. This motion is used when a member doubts the result of a vote announced by the chair. A division must be called for before the chair states another motion. If a member wants the vote to be counted, he or she must make a motion to that effect.

Forms of the Motion

"I call for a division."

"Division."

Rules Governing the Motion

1. Can interrupt a speaker

2. Does not require recognition

3. Is not debatable

4. Is not amendable

5. Does not require a vote, since a single member can demand that a vote be taken by standing

Division of the Question

An incidental motion. The purpose of this motion is to divide a motion or an amendment if it consists of two or more parts, each part being capable of standing alone.

The motion must state clearly the manner in which the question is to be divided. A motion cannot be divided unless each part presents a proper question for the assembly to act on if none of the other parts is adopted. A resolution cannot be divided if it contains several parts which would be impossible to separate without rewriting the resolution.

Forms of the Motion

"I move to divide the motion so as to consider separately the . . . and the . . . ."

"I move to divide the resolution so as to consider separately the question on . . . and the question on . . . ."

Rules Governing the Motion

1. Cannot interrupt a speaker
2. Requires recognition
3. Requires a second
4. Is not debatable
5. Is amendable
6. Requires a majority vote
7. Cannot be reconsidered

Lay on the Table
(Temporarily)

A subsidiary motion. This motion puts aside the pending question temporarily when something more urgent arises. The motion to lay on the table cannot be qualified in any way. The motion to use is to postpone to a certain time.

When the motion is laid on the table, all adhering motions go with it. When taken from the table, the motion comes back exactly as it was, with all the adhering motions.

The motion to lay on the table may be taken from the table on the same day, provided that some other business has taken place. If the motion is not taken from the table at the close of the next regular business meeting, the question dies. However, the matter can be taken up as new business at a later meeting.

Forms of the Motion

"I move to lay the question on the table."

"I move that the resolution be laid on the table."

Rules Governing the Motion

1. Cannot interrupt a speaker

2. Requires recognition

3. Requires a second

4. Is not debatable; however, a member may make a short statement as to the reason for making the motion

5. Is not amendable

6. Requires a majority vote

Limit or Extend Debate

A subsidiary motion. This motion is to limit the time that will be devoted to the discussion of a pending question, or to lengthen the time of discussion.

Forms of the Motion

"I move to limit debate on the motion to one hour."

"I move to limit the time of each speaker on the motion to three minutes."

"I move that the time of the speaker be extended by ten minutes."

Rules Governing the Motion

1. Cannot interrupt a speaker

2. Requires recognition

3. Is not debatable

4. Is amendable only as to time

5. Requires a two-thirds vote

6. Can be reconsidered

Main Motion

The main motion brings a subject before the assembly for its discussion and decision.

Motions that can be made while the main motion is pending include: all subsidiary and all privileged motions; and applicable incidental motions, such as: division of the question, consider by paragraph, withdraw, object to the consideration of an original main motion.

A main motion should be stated in the affirmative, since the negative form often confuses members in voting. Avoid saying, "I move that we do not increase our dues." The motion can be clearly stated by saying, "I move that our dues remain the same." A main motion should be concise, clear, and made as complete as possible so as to avoid amendments.

Forms of the Motion

"I move that we establish a scholarship fund."

"I move the adoption of the following resolution, RESOLVED: That . . . ."

Rules Governing the Motion

1. Cannot interrupt a speaker

2. Requires recognition

3. Requires a second

4. Is debatable

5. Is amendable

6. Yields to all subsidiary, privileged, or applicable incidental motions

7. Requires a majority vote, except when the bylaws require a greater vote; when adoption would have the effect of suspending a rule of order or a parliamentary right; or when adoption would have the effect of rescinding or amending something previously adopted

8. May be reconsidered

Method of Voting

An incidental motion. This motion is used when some form other than voice vote is desired.

Form of the Motion

"I move that when we vote, we vote by ballot."

Rules Governing the Motion

1. Cannot interrupt a speaker

2. Requires recognition

3. Requires a second

4. Is not debatable

5. Is amendable

6. Requires a majority vote

Object to the Consideration of a Question

An incidental motion. This motion is used to avoid a particular embarrassing or undesirable original main motion from being discussed. If an objection is sustained, the motion is not before the assembly.

Form of the Motion

"I object to the consideration of the motion (resolution)."

Rules Governing the Motion

1. Can interrupt proceedings; must be made before the chair states the motion and before any debate
2. Does not require a second
3. Is not debatable
4. Is not amendable
5. Requires two-thirds vote against consideration to sustain the objection

Parliamentary Inquiry

An incidental motion. The purpose of this motion is to enable a member to ask the chair a question of procedure in connection with the pending question or with a motion that the member wishes to bring before the assembly immediately. It is also used to ask for information on the effect of the pending question.

Form of the Motion

"I rise to a parliamentary inquiry."

Rules Governing the Motion

1. Can interrupt a speaker if it requires an immediate answer

2. Requires no second

3. Is not debatable

4. Is not amendable

5. Requires no vote

6. Can have no motion applied to it

Point of Order

An incidental motion. This motion is to call to the attention of the chair a violation of a rule when the chair neglects to call it.

A point of order must be raised immediately. It cannot be brought up later unless the error involved a violation of the bylaws. The motion interrupts business. The presiding officer either rules that the point of order is well taken and orders the mistake or omission to be corrected, or rules that the point of order is not well taken and resumes business at the point where it was interrupted.

Forms of the Motion

"I rise to a point of order."

"Point of order."

Rules Governing the Motion

1. Can interrupt a speaker

2. Does not require recognition

3. Does not require a second

4. Is not debatable

5. Is not amendable

6. Does not require a vote as the chair decides; if submitted to the assembly, a majority vote is required

7. May not be reconsidered

Postpone Definitely (to a Certain Time)

A subsidiary motion. This is a motion by which action on a pending question can be put off, within limits, to a definite day, meeting, or hour, or until a certain event.

There are limits on postponement. A question can be postponed only until the close of the next session. In a convention, a motion may not be postponed beyond the last meeting of the convention.

Forms of the Motion

"I move to postpone consideration of the motion until 3 P.M."

"I move to postpone the question until our next meeting."

"I move to postpone consideration of this question until our next meeting, and that it be made a special order for 1:30 P.M."

Rules Governing the Motion

1. Cannot interrupt a speaker

2. Requires recognition

3. Requires a second

4. Is debatable only as to the propriety and details of postponement

5. Is amendable only as to time to which the question is to be postponed

6. Requires a majority vote in its simple form; requires a two-thirds vote if made a special order

7. Can be reconsidered

Previous Question (Stop Debate)

A subsidiary motion. The motion "previous question" is often misunderstood. It is a motion to stop debate and take an immediate vote on the pending question. Members sometimes call out "Question" without obtaining the floor. This is discourteous and disorderly.

If the previous question is adopted, votes are taken immediately on the question specified. If lost, debate continues on the immediately pending question.

Forms of the Motion

"I move to vote immediately on the motion."

"I move to vote now on all pending questions."

"I move the previous question."

Rules Governing the Motion

1. Cannot interrupt a speaker

2. Requires recognition

3. Requires a second

4. Is not debatable

5. Is not amendable

6. Requires a two-thirds vote

Question of Privilege

A privileged motion. This motion enables a member to secure immediate decision and action by the presiding officer on a request that concerns the comfort, convenience, rights, or privileges of the assembly or of the member. It is also used to request permission to present a motion of urgent nature, even though business is pending.

Forms of the Motion

"I rise to a question of privilege of the assembly."

"I rise to a question of personal privilege."

Rules Governing the Motion

1. Can interrupt a speaker if it requires an immediate answer

2. Does not require recognition

3. Is not debatable

4. Is not amendable

5. Requires no vote

6. Chair rules; ruling is subject to appeal

7. May not be reconsidered

8. Can have no motion applied to it except the motion to withdraw

Ratify

A specific main motion. To ratify means to approve, confirm, validate, or make legal. The object of the motion is to approve or legalize an action taken in an emergency or when no quorum was present.

Forms of the Motion

"I move to ratify the action taken by the executive committee."

"I move that we ratify the action taken by . . . ."

Action already taken cannot become legally valid until approved by the assembly. The assembly can ratify such actions of its officers, committees, and delegates as it would have the right to authorize in advance. It cannot make valid a voice vote election when the bylaws require elections by ballot, nor can it ratify anything done in violation of national, state, or local law.

Rules Governing the Motion

1. Cannot interrupt a speaker

2. Requires recognition

3. Requires a second

4. Is debatable

5. Is amendable

6. Requires a majority vote

7. Can be reconsidered

Recess

A privileged motion. Recess is a short intermission in the assembly's proceedings which does not close the meeting, and after which business will be resumed at exactly where it was interrupted.

When a motion to recess is made when no business is pending, it is a main motion. When a recess is provided for in the adopted program, the chair, without further action by the assembly, announces the fact and declares the assembly to be in recess when that time comes. If the chair fails to announce the recess at that time, a member may call for the orders of the day.

Forms of the Motion

"I move that we recess for ten minutes."

"I move to recess until 2:30 P.M."

Rules Governing the Motion

1. Cannot interrupt a speaker

2. Requires recognition

3. Requires a second

4. Is not debatable

5. Is amendable as to the length of time of the recess

6. Requires a majority vote

7. May be reconsidered

Reconsider

A specific main motion. The purpose of the motion to reconsider a vote taken on a motion is to bring that motion again before the assembly, as though no vote had been taken on it.

The motion to reconsider can be made only on the same day or the next calendar day after the original vote was taken.

Form of the Motion

"I move to reconsider the vote taken on the motion relating to . . . ."

Rules Governing the Motion

1. Cannot interrupt a speaker

2. Requires recognition

3. Requires a second

4. Is debatable

5. Is not amendable

6. Requires a majority vote

7. Cannot be reconsidered

Rescind

A specific main motion. The purpose of the motion is to repeal (cancel, void) a main motion passed at a previous meeting. The effect of the motion to rescind is to strike out an entire motion, resolution, rule, or paragraph that has been adopted at some previous meeting. However, there is some action which cannot be rescinded. When something has been done as a result of a vote on the motion, it is impossible to undo it.

Form of the Motion

"I move to rescind the motion passed at the May meeting concerning . . . ."

Rules Governing the Motion

1. Cannot interrupt a speaker

2. Requires recognition

3. Requires a second

4. Is debatable and opens the motion it proposes to rescind to debate

5. Cannot be amended

6. Requires a majority vote with previous notice

Suspend the Rules

An incidental motion. This motion is used when the assembly wishes to do something that cannot be done without violating its own rules, but which does not conflict with the constitution or bylaws, local, state, or national laws, or with the fundamental rules of parliamentary procedure.

Rules that may not be suspended include: rules contained in the bylaws, constitution, or charter, unless that particular document specifies for its own suspension; rules protecting absentees or basic rights of the individual members.

Rules that may be suspended include: rules of order (parliamentary procedure) by a two-thirds vote; standing rules (rules that do not relate to parliamentary procedure, such as hours for meetings to begin or end).

Forms of the Motion

"I move to suspend rule number five."

"I move to suspend the rule which interferes with . . . ."

"I move to suspend the rule in order to take up . . . ."

Rules Governing the Motion

1. Cannot interrupt a speaker

2. Requires recognition

3. Requires a second

4. Is not debatable

5. Is not amendable

6. Requires a two-thirds vote

7. Can have no motions applied to it except to withdraw

8. Must be decided immediately

Take from the Table

A specific main motion. This motion is used when it is desired to bring back for further consideration a motion that was laid on the table.

Forms of the Motion

"I move to take from the table the motion relating to . . . ."

Rules Governing the Motion

1. Cannot interrupt a speaker
2. Requires recognition
3. Requires a second
4. Is not debatable
5. Is not amendable
6. Requires a majority vote
7. Cannot be reconsidered

Withdraw a Motion

An incidental motion. This motion allows a member who proposed a motion to remove it from consideration by the assembly. The consent of the seconder is not necessary. A motion can be withdrawn if there is no objection, or with permission from the assembly, up to the moment the final vote is taken.

Forms of the Motion

"I withdraw my motion." (before the motion has been stated by the chair)

"I request permission to withdraw my motion." (after the motion has been stated and discussed)

Rules Governing the Motion

1. Cannot interrupt a speaker

2. Requires recognition

3. Requires no second, as it is a request

4. Is not debatable

5. Is not amendable

6. Requires no vote

7. Can apply to all motions

Index

A

Ad hoc committee, 18
Adjournment
  motion for, 50–52
    forms of, 50
    rules governing, 51–52
Adoption
  motion for, 52
    forms of, 52
    rules governing, 52
Advisory committee, 19
Advisory council, 19
Agenda, 26–27
  in board meeting, 26–27
  in committees, 7
Amendment(s)
  motions for, 53–54
    forms of, 53
    rules governing for, 54
  motion for previously adopted
    action, 54–55
    forms of motion for, 55
    rules governing motion for,
      55
Appeal
  motion for, 55–56
    form of, 56
    rules governing, 56
Appointment
  by the chair, 4
  by the presiding officer, 4
Assembly, division of, 63–64
  forms of motion for, 64
  rules governing motion for, 64
Auditing committee, 20

B

Ballot, nominations by, 5–6
Board of directors, 2
  conducting meetings, 26–28
    agendas, 26–27
    board reports, 29
    meeting by telephone, 28–29
    other materials, 27–28
  definition of, 23
  establishing, 23–24
  functions of, 24
  officers of, 25–26
  responsibilities of, 24–25
  small, 28
Board reports, 29
Body, 32–33
Budget committee, 16–18

C

Call for orders of the day, 56–57
  form of motion for, 57
  rules governing motion for, 57
Chair
  appointment by, 4
  nominations by, 4–5
Close of debate, 57–58
  forms of motion for, 58
  rules governing motion for, 58
Close of nominations, 58–59
  form of motion to, 59
  rules governing motion to, 59
Commit
  motion for, 59–60
    forms of, 59–60

rules governing motion to, 60

Committees, 1-2
agendas, 7
conducting business, 6-7
discharging of, 9-10, 62-63
executive, 24
functions of, 2-3
kinds of, 2
rules governing, 6-7
selecting, 4-6
size of, 3
special, 18-22
advisory, 19
auditing, 20
credentials, 21-22
nominating, 19
subcommittees, 18
standing, 15
budget committee, 16-18
Committee chair
effective, 11-12
responsibilities of, 12-13
rules regarding, 13
Committee discharge
forms of motion for, 62-63
rules governing motion for, 63
Committee members, 7-9
ex-officio, 8, 25
observers, 8-9
Committee report
disposition of, 25-26
minority view, 24-25
oral reports, 23-24
preparing, 21-22
presenting, 24
written, 22-23
Consideration by paragraph, 61-62
forms of motion for, 61
rules governing motion for, 62
Consider informally
motion for, 60-61
form of, 60
rules governing, 60

Courtesy resolution, 41
Credentials committee, 21-22

D
Debate
motion to extend, 67
form of, 67
rules governing, 67
motion to limit, 67
form of, 67
rules governing, 67
Directors, 23. *See also* Board of directors
Discharge of committee motion
forms of, 62-63
rules governing, 63
Division of the assembly
motion, 63-64
forms of, 64
rules governing, 64

E
Estimated expenditures, 16
Executive committee, 24
Ex-officio members, 8, 25
president as, of committees/boards, 8
Extend debate, 67
form of motion to, 67
rules governing motion to, 67

F
Floor
nominations from, 5

H
Heading, 22

I
Incidental motion, 48
Income budget, 16
Informal consideration, 60-61
form of motion for, 60
rules governing motion for, 60-61

J
Joint committee, 18

L
Lay on table, 65–66
  form of motion to, 66
  rules governing motion to, 66
Limit debate, 67
  form of motion to, 67
  rules governing motion to, 67

M
Main motions, 38–39, 68–69
  forms of, 68
  rules governing, 68–69
Members, ex-officio, 8, 25
Method of voting
  forms of motion for, 69
  rules governing motion for, 69
Minority view, 24–25
Minutes, 29
Motions, 37–41
  adjournment, 50–52
    forms of, 50
    rules governing, 51–52
  adoption, 52
    forms of, 52
    rules governing, 52
  to amend, 53–54
    forms of, 53
    rules governing, 54
  to amend previously adopted
      action, 54–55
    forms of motion, 55
    rules governing, 55
  for appeal, 55–56
    form of, 56
    rules governing, 56
  call for the orders of the day,
      56–57
    form of, 57
    rules governing, 57
  to close debate, 57–58
    forms of, 58
    rules governing, 58

  to close nominations
    form of motion to, 59
    rules governing, 59
  commit, 59
    form of motion to, 59–60
    rules governing motion to,
      60
  consider by paragraph, 61–62
    form of motion to, 61
    rules governing motion to,
      62
  consider informally, 60–61
    form of motion to, 60
    rules governing motion to,
      60
  courtesy resolution, 40
  discharge a committee, 62
    forms of, 62–63
    rules governing, 63
  division of the assembly,
      63–64
    forms of, 64
    rules governing, 64
  extend debate, 67
    form of, 67
    rules governing, 67
  incidental, 48
  kinds of, 37–38
  lay on table, 65–66
    form of, 66
    rules governing, 66
  limit debate, 67
    form of, 67
    rules governing, 67
  main, 38–39, 68–69
    forms of, 68
    rules governing, 68–69
  method of voting, 69
    forms of, 69
    rules governing, 69
  objection to consideration of
      question, 70
    forms of, 70
    rules governing, 70
  parliamentary inquiry, 70–71

forms of, 71
rules governing, 71
point of order, 71–72
forms of, 72
rules governing, 72
postpone definitely (to a
certain time), 72–73
form of, 73
rules governing, 73
precedence of, 41, 49–50
previous question, 74
forms of, 74
rules governing, 74
primary, 37–38, 47
privileged, 39, 47–48
question of privilege, 75
forms of, 75
rules governing, 75
ratification, 76
forms of, 76
rules governing, 76
recess, 77
form of, 77
rules governing, 77
reconsider, 78
form of, 78
rules governing, 78
refer, 59–60
form of, 59–60
rules governing, 60
rescind, 78–79
form of, 79
rules governing, 79
resolutions, 39–40
secondary, 37–38, 47
subsidiary, 39, 41
suspend the rules, 79–80
form of, 80
rules governing, 80
take from table, 81
form of, 81
rules governing, 81
withdraw, 81–82
form of, 82
rules governing, 82

N
Nominating committee, 19
Nominations
by ballot, 5–6
from the floor, 5
motion to close, 58–59
form of, 59
rules governing, 59

O
Objection to consideration of
question, 70
forms of motion for, 70
rules governing motion for, 70
Observers, 8–9
Opinions, 21
Ordinary committees, 2

P
Parliamentary inquiry, 70–71
forms of motion for, 71
rules governing motion for, 71
Point of order, 71–72
forms of motion for, 72
rules governing motion for, 72
Postpone definitely (to a certain
time), 72–73
form of motion to, 73
rules governing motion to, 73
Preamble, 40
Presiding officer
appointment by, 4
nominations by, 4–5
Previous question, 74
forms of motion for, 74
rules governing motion for, 74
Primary motions, 37–38, 47
Privileged motion, 39, 47–48
Proxy, vote by, 25

Q
Question
motion on division of
forms of, 65
rules governing, 65

motion objecting to
consideration of, 70
forms of, 70
rules governing, 70
motion of privilege, 75
forms of, 75
rules governing, 75
Quorum
for board of directors, 25
for committee meeting, 8

R
Ratification, 76
forms of motion for, 76
rules governing motion for, 76
Recess
motion for, 77
form of, 77
rules governing, 77
Reconsider
motion for, 78
form of, 78
rules governing, 78
Refer
motion for, 59–60
forms of, 59–60
rules governing, 60
Registration, 22
Rescind
motion for, 78–79
form of, 79
rules governing, 79
Resolutions, 39–40
Rules. *See also under individual
motions*
governing committees, 6–7
motion to suspend, 79–80

S
Secondary motions, 37–38, 47
Signature, 23

Special committees, 2, 18–22
advisory, 19
auditing, 20
credentials, 21–22
nominating, 19
subcommittees, 18
Standing committees, 2, 15
budget, 16–18
Studies, 21
Subcommittees, 18
Subsidiary motions, 39, 41, 47
Surveys, 21
Suspend the rules
motion for, 79–80
form of, 80
rules governing, 80

T
Take from table
motion for, 80
form of, 81
rules governing, 81
Telephone, meeting by, 28–29

V
Voting
method of, 69
forms of motion for, 69
rules governing motion for,
69

W
Withdrawal of motion, 81–82
forms of, 82
rules governing, 82
Written reports, 22–23

NTC COMMUNICATION BOOKS

Speech Communication
The Basics of Speech, *Galvin, Cooper, & Gordon*
  The Basics of Speech Workbook, *Galvin & Cooper*
Contemporary Speech, *HopKins & Whitaker*
Creative Speaking, *Buys et al.*
  Creative Speaking Series
Dynamics of Speech, *Myers & Herndon*
Getting Started in Public Speaking, *Prentice & Payne*
Listening by Doing, *Galvin*
Literature Alive! *Gamble & Gamble*
Person to Person, *Galvin & Book*
  Person to Person Workbook, *Galvin & Book*
Self-Awareness, *Ratliffe & Herman*
Speaking by Doing, *Buys, Sills, & Beck*

Business Communication
Business Communication Today! *Thomas & Fryar*
Effective Group Communication, *Ratliffe & Stech*
Handbook for Business Writing, *Baugh, Fryar, & Thomas*
Meetings, *Pohl*
Successful Business Speaking, *Fryar & Thomas*
Successful Business Writing, Sitzmann
Successful Interviewing, *Sitzmann & Garcia*
Successful Problem Solving, *Fryar & Thomas*
Working in Groups, *Ratliffe & Stech*

For a current catalog and information about our complete line
of language arts books, write:
National Textbook Company,
a division of NTC Publishing Group
4255 West Touhy Avenue
Lincolnwood (Chicago), Illinois 60646-1975 U.S.A.